Nicholas Murray

BLOOMSBURY AND THE POETS

Bruce Chatwin
A Life of Matthew Arnold
After Arnold: Culture and Accessibility
World Enough and Time: The Life of Andrew Marvell
Aldous Huxley: An English Intellectual
Kafka
So Spirited a Town: Visions and Versions of Liverpool
A Corkscrew is Most Useful: The Travellers of Empire
Real Bloomsbury
The Red Sweet Wine of Youth:
British Poets of the First World War

FICTION
A Short Book About Love
Remembering Carmen

POETRY
Plausible Fictions
The Narrators
Get Real!
Acapulco: New and Selected Poems
Of earth, water, air and fire: animal poems
Trench Feet

AS CONTRIBUTOR
Other People's Clerihews
Art for All? Their Policies and Our Culture
Sybille Bedford: In Memory
Malcolm Lowry: from the Mersey to the world

Nicholas Murray

BLOOMSBURY
AND THE POETS

Rack Press Editions

Rack Press Editions is an imprint of Rack Press Poetry

Typeset by CB editions, London
Printed by Berforts Information Press, Oxford

Published in Wales by Rack Press,
The Rack, Kinnerton, Presteigne, Powys, LD8 2PF
Tel: 01547 560 411
All orders and correspondence:
rackpress@nicholasmurray.co.uk

ISBN 978-0-9927654-6-0

Contents

Bloomsbury and the Poets

Who's afraid of W.C.1?

'My God how workmen smell!' Vita Sackville-West exploded when the central heating installers had finally left her Kent home in 1927.

'I hate the proletariat.'[1]

Vita was a friend of Virginia Woolf and thus an honorary member of 'Bloomsbury', a district of London widely suspected by its detractors of specialising in such snobbish views of the populace.

Taken with some languidly arrogant *bon mots* from Lytton Strachey, an injudicious remark or two from Virginia Woolf (whose affair with Vita lay behind her splendidly inventive novel *Orlando*), any number of haughty absurdities dropped by the well-born aesthetes, and one has it: the insufferable toffs prevailed in this quarter of London and decent people should breathe contentedly in the knowledge that they live at the furthest possible distance from such types.

It was therefore with confidence in a ready audience that the poet Dylan Thomas spoke for the common man and woman when he sneered at 'the shams and shamans, the amateur hobo and homo of Bloomsbury, W.C.1'.[2]

The toffs, however, saw it differently. When Virginia and Vanessa Stephen – always insistent that they were not actually posh at all – first arrived at No. 46 Gordon Square, Bloomsbury, in 1904 from their father's house at Hyde Park Gate, their relatives were appalled.

'It was a cold, grim house in a cold, grim district,'[3] a disconcerted Harold Nicholson observed of the stuccoed building, overlooking the carefully untended greenery of the Square, a property that most present day house-hunters would ache to possess. But Bloomsbury at the turn of the nineteenth century was very far from being the desirable location it can seem today. Henry James called it at this moment in its history 'dirty Bloomsbury'.[4]

Ford Madox Ford evoked a 'Bloomsbury of dismal, decorous, unhappy, glamorous squares',[5] and V. S. Pritchett wrote of the 'spiritless streets of Bloomsbury'.[6]

In contrast to the *beau idéal* of society May-
fair, this district with its worthy educational
institutions and hospitals, its seedy Bohemian-
ism, was most definitely out of fashion. Even
the characteristic Georgian squares were shab-
by and neglected for the most part, consisting
very often of lodging houses filled with indigent
writers, lawyers, actors and yet more doubtful
characters.

Music hall jokes featured the figure of The
Bloomsbury Landlady who managed these
seedy accommodations and it was no surprise
that efforts were made on the part of their relatives to make the Stephen girls see their folly.

As late as 1966, the spikily controversial architectural writer Ian Nairn, in his book *Nairn's
London*, could write that: 'As anything more than
an area on a map, Bloomsbury is dead. Town
planners and London University have killed it
between them – a notable academic victory.'[7]

Today the vast battery-hen hotels of the Im-
perial group out of which issue chattering flocks
of Euro-teenagers on their way to dutiful tours
of the British Museum and later Big Ben, make
Bloomsbury, once the vast student population
has been added in, more populated and lively

than it was in its Edwardian period but it has never managed to fulfil the dreams cherished by the early nineteenth-century speculative builders and the Bedford Estate of an elegant aristocratic residential quarter to rival Belgravia.

Back in 1904, however, Virginia Stephen was determined to make the most of her escape from the suffocating gentility and the upper middle class sterility of her late Victorian family home. As her sister Vanessa later observed: 'It was in these years . . . that there came the great expansion and development of Bloomsbury, that life seemed fullest of interest and promise and expansion of all kinds.'[8]

The Zulu of Regent Square

E arly in 1921 the South African born poet
and bruiser Roy Campbell found himself
– very probably to his own surprise – sharing a
house in Regent Square, Bloomsbury with what
he plainly considered a group of rather effete
young literary intellectuals including Aldous
Huxley, Thomas W. Earp (allegedly the source
of the word 'twerp') and Russell Green.

For Campbell, his flatmate Huxley was no
more than 'a pedant who leeringly gloated
over his knowledge of how crayfish copulated
(through their third pair of legs) but could never have cooked one, let alone broken in a horse,
thrown and branded a steer, flensed a whale, or
slaughtered, cut, cured, and cooked anything at
all'.[9]

This seems rather unfair on Huxley and his
friends, opportunities for breaking in horses and
branding steers, let alone flensing whales, surely

presenting themselves as few in the streets of Bloomsbury. Campbell called himself 'the Zulu' and given his pugnacious *machismo* (he punched at various times, in pubs or poetry readings, Stephen Spender and Louis MacNeice) and his self-image as a rough outdoor, bull-fighting, farmer and flenser, it is hard to see what he was actually doing in a residential district of London whose presiding spirits were Virginia Woolf and Lytton Strachey.

The publisher's blurb on the jacket of Campbell's last book, *Portugal*, published in 1957 and finished only weeks before his death, shows the Campbell myth fully intact: 'In the course of his vigorous life, which ended so tragically when he was killed in a motor-accident in May, 1957, he was professional bull-fighter and wandering circus performer in Provence, a fisherman off the southern coast of France, a soldier in both World Wars . . .'

The book itself glorifies the 'inspired' leadership of the Portuguese dictator Salazar (a 'statesman of peasant stock') and attacks 'the Reds' such as Koestler, Hemingway and Spender who, Campbell claimed with satisfaction, had been seen off.

Small wonder that Campbell, in 1931, would publish 'a satirical fantasy in verse' called *The Georgiad*,[10] that attempted to scourge in rhyming couplets what he saw as the comfortably cliquish Georgian poets and those of the 1920s and 1930s who were in the ascendant in Bloomsbury and beyond.

Campbell was a genuine poet whose versions of the great Spanish mystic, St John of the Cross, are still admired but this satire badly needs the light, agile step and thrust of the *picador* that he claimed to be. He had a good subject and some tempting targets but as the couplets unroll, even allowing for the passage of 80 years and the inevitable obscurity of some of the contemporary references, the reader waits in vain for some really focused and vivid poetic writing, some memorable images. He mocks the Bloomsbury accent ('Between its tonsils drawing out long O's/ Along its draughty, supercilious nose'), the weekend ruralism of the 'meek' Georgian poets ('The Stately Homes of England ope their doors/ To piping Nancy-boys and crashing Bores,/ Where for week-ends the scavengers of letters/ Convene to chew the fat about their betters'), the vegetarians, advocates of 'free love', political

7

progressives, homosexuals and androgynes, the (unspecified) 'Bloomsbury matriarchies' who are judged responsible for manipulating reputations, the literary dinners ('Where I have suffered, choked with evening dress/ And ogled by some frosty poetess'), and all the effete, bloodless, sexless 'intellectuals without intellect' who populate the reactionary Campbell's nightmare Bloomsbury.

The house at No. 36 Regent Square no longer exists. There is no facade to be stamped with a blue plaque, that northern side of the Square having been rebuilt after the war with featureless public housing blocks. On the south side, however, a few Georgian houses remain to give an idea of what No. 36 probably looked like.

This north-eastern corner of Bloomsbury never has been the most fashionable part of the district. Wander out of Regent Square into the network of streets that give access to the multi-ethnic area of Cromer Street, then stroll northwards towards King's Cross, and you will soon find yourself at Argyll Square. Once a sleazy red light district, the gentrification of St Pancras International station, the tarting up of King's Cross Station, and the luxury refurbishment of the St Pancras Hotel have displaced the sex workers further east. As a result, Argyll Square has lost its former reputation.

The poet Arthur Rimbaud stayed here, at No. 12, with his mother and sister, Vitalie, in July 1874 before vanishing – no one knows where – on the morning of July 31st. Vitalie's *Voyage à Londres*, which is reproduced in the Pléiade edition of Rimbaud's works,[11] has the freshness of a young woman's observation of a country and a city new to her.

Arthur, who is always assumed to have been hard at work polishing his disreputable image, seems to have been, for this week at least, the perfect son and elder brother, patiently accompanying his family on their exploration of the shops and the sights. The weather was very hot that July. 'Arthur is so very kind,' Vitalie wrote one sweltering day. 'I was longing to treat myself to an ice, and Arthur anticipated my desire.'

It was of course further north, at No. 8 Royal College Street in Camden where, a year earlier, in the summer of 1873, Rimbaud had been shot in the arm in a lover's tiff with the poet Verlaine. But that is another story. The Bloomsbury poets may have bored each other but they did not resort to firearms. Camden Town remains to this day a wilder, raunchier place.

Ambiguous types

J ean Cocteau, in some notes on Paris written in 1941 but not published until 2013, was one of the first to propose the now hackneyed idea of the city as a cluster of villages (*'Paris est une grande ville, faite de petites villages et de villages que même les étrangers connaissent mieux que nous'*).[12] He considered his own rather posh patch around the Grand Palais as having the tiny parochial life of a small village street (*'Tout est affaire de quartier chez nous'*).

But he also captured the other side of this cosy intimacy: the city's rapacious gobbling up of lives, its ruthlessness, its implacability: 'Paris has the stomach of an ostrich; it swallows everything but retains nothing.' (*'Paris possède un estomac d'autruche. Il digère tout. Il n'assimile rien'*).

One such *quartier* is Marchmont Street, a street of which Virginia Woolf was especially fond, using it as Bloomsbury residents still do today, as a place to get ordinary bits and pieces of household stuff. 'Oh, the convenience of the place and the loveliness too,' she told her diary in April 1924. 'Why do I love it so much?'[13]

A fair question, one might think. Unlike, say, Lamb's Conduit Street a few minutes' walk away, heavily gentrified with pretty and impossibly expensive shops, Marchmont Street's charms are of the scruffy kind. It has stores selling cheap household items, a halal butcher, a building supplier, a cheap Chinese restaurant (though Charles's, with its unadorned Greek menu, and its slow-moving lone proprietor, who still lives in the basement, is long gone) an Afghan vegetable stall, and a gay bookshop. Gentrification has started but it hasn't yet begun to tilt the balance of the street.

The poet William Empson turned up here in the summer of 1929. Not quite as badly behaved as Arthur Rimbaud, but fond of a drink, particularly across the Bloomsbury border into Soho and Fitzrovia, Empson had just been kicked out of Cambridge after contraceptives were found in his undergraduate room. For two years he rented rooms for 28 shillings a week at No. 65 (now the New Bloomsbury Halal Bangladeshi butcher) where he completed one of the most celebrated works of twentieth-century literary criticism, *Seven Types of Ambiguity*. Confessing to the other famous Cambridge literary critic, I. A. Richards, that he had 'a taste for squalor and cooking my own meals',[14] Empson went on to update Richards about the book's progress (60,000 words by this time). He was worried that he would not get it published: 'I am much hampered by a doubt as to whether any of it is true.'

One June afternoon in 2011 a little knot of *literati*, dons from London University, writers from the *Times Literary Supplement*, the Street's energetic historian and spinner of blue plaques Ricci De Freitas, members of the Empson family, and the present writer gathered to watch a plaque being unveiled to the former bad boy turned knight of the realm. Tourists passed by, baffled by the show of interest in someone they had never heard of.

No. 65 was owned by an unconventional hospital consultant called Gilbert Back whose wife later married the poet Edgell Rickword. A friend of Empson's reported that the poet 'is living in Bloomsbury in a large room, beautifully furnished above the waist-level, below a sea of books, bread, hair-brushes and dirty towels.'[15]

Another visitor, the poet and novelist Sylvia Townsend Warner reported on an invitation to supper at No. 65: 'I had gone a little frightened, fearing it might be a party of intellectual young things; but it was as though he had foreseen that I was a timid grandmother, for when I arrived it was to a very untidy room, with bottles and books on the floor, a delicious smell of frying, a saucepan of twopenny soup on a gas-ring and Mr Empson cavalier seul. So nothing could have been pleasanter. He had learned to cook because his sister runs Girl Guides.'[16]

Strolling across Russell Square one day, almost certainly on his way to a Soho watering-hole, Empson collided with T. S. Eliot, Bloomsbury's supreme poetic presence as Poetry Editor at the publisher Faber and Faber, located in the Square's corner, a few minutes' walk from Marchmont Street. Empson quizzed the great poet about a recent opinion he had given, in the preface to a collection of poems by Ezra Pound, that a poet should be constantly writing, preferably producing one poem a week.

With the dry, magisterial suavity that was his

speciality Eliot thoughtfully revised his earlier opinion: 'Taking the question in general,' he told Empson, 'I should say, in the case of many poets, that the most important thing for them to do . . . is to write as little as possible.'

Eliot's papal court was at No. 24 Russell Square, as a brown Camden Council plaque records. London's plaques can be confusing. The classic blue ones, once but no longer administered by English Heritage, are joined by local council efforts as here, as well as by a scatter of independent freelance plaques and plates and notices. In the deregulated plaque free-for-all local associations have not been slothful, and the Marchmont Association has been responsible for a sprinkling of blue ones in and around the Street. Until the blue disk went up recently we all had no idea that Lenin had stopped ever so briefly in Tavistock Place, along Virginia Woolf's shopping route from home in Tavistock Square to Marchmont Street.

Eliot worked from 1925 to 1965 in what is now known as The Faber Building (the publishers later moved to Queen Square and have now come to rest in an elegant building in Great Russell Street). His mentally ill first wife, Vivienne

Haigh-Wood, used to cram bars of chocolate through the letter-box because she was convinced that he was imprisoned inside and being starved to death. In fact he was well-fed, at least on Wednesdays, when Faber's caretaker, Mr Tansley, who lived with his wife in the attic and who had been poisoned by mustard gas in the First World War, served up in the boardroom to the Faber directors a good solid English lunch of meat and two veg.

Reflecting on the bitter experience of his first marriage – its handling by Eliot still a matter of controversy, as the play by Michael Hastings and later film *Tom and Viv* suggest – the poet observed: 'To her, the marriage brought no happiness. To me, it brought the state of mind out of which came *The Waste Land*.'[17]

The eastern side of Russell Square is dominated by the massively ornate facade of the once rather *louche* 1890s Russell Hotel in red brick and terracotta and it was here that Eliot brought his Faber secretary, Valerie Fletcher, thirty years his junior, for drinks after work. She was soon to become the second Mrs Eliot. Some unpublished drafts of Eliot's *Old Possum's Book of Practical Cats* make reference to the hotel.

As one leaves Russell Square's south east corner it is easy to miss, at the foot of a youthful Irish Yew shooting up from a thicket of lesser but invasive foliage, a metal plaque which explains that in May 1996 the Worshipful Mayor of Camden, together with Valerie Eliot, watched His Excellency the High Commissioner for India in the United Kingdom, Dr L. M. Singhvi, plant this *taxus baccata 'Fastigiara'* in remembrance of the poet.

If we follow Empson out of Russell Square on his way to Soho/Fitzrovia to the west, we pass under the grey tower of Senate House, reputedly Orwell's model for the Ministry of Truth in *Nineteen Eighty-Four*, and also rumoured to have been Hitler's office HQ of choice should he have succeeded in invading Britain. Here, during World War Two, several poets such as Dylan Thomas and Louis MacNeice worked in the Ministry of Information which had commandeered the building for the war effort.

Louis MacNeice wrote several poems about Bloomsbury, the best of which is probably 'October in Bloomsbury' published in 1962. The poem brings us to contemplate the statue of Charles James Fox which, situated at the

northern extremity of Bloomsbury Square, looks
along the majestic straight of Bedford Place to
encounter the gaze of fellow Whig Francis Russell, fifth Duke of Bedford. MacNeice describes
Fox who 'unconcerned in a bath towel sits on
his arse in Bloomsbury Square/ While plane
tree leaves flop gently down and lodge in his
sculptured hair'.[18]

More recently, the poet Christopher Reid in
The Song of Lunch (2009) has his protagonist
leaving a Bloomsbury publisher's office to re-
flect that the area is 'a district of literary ghosts/
that walk in broad daylight'.[19] Reid is a former
Poetry Editor of Faber whose offices were, in his
day, in Queen Square and such thoughts must
often have gone through his mind when arriv-
ing at the office.

The Cockney rabble

I f you were to leave Russell Square in its north-western corner, passing the Faber Building and taking that very pleasant walk through one of Bloomsbury's quieter and more peaceful squares, Woburn Square, you would soon find yourself at Gordon Square, much larger and more park-like, overlooked by the former Woolf home and containing a relatively recent addition, a statue of the Bengali poet Rabindranath Tagore, the first non-European to win the Nobel Prize.

Running down the western side of Gordon Square is Gordon Street, where the poet Arthur Hugh Clough in 1849 became the first Principal of the Unitarian University Hall, designed to house the dissenting students at the new University College. Clough was caught up in the early Victorian drama of Faith and Doubt but the appointment to University Hall (now

Dr Williams's Library of Dissent) failed to save him from Doubt's torments and he soon quit. Gordon Street, however, was for many years the home of another poet who deserves far more recognition.

The 'godless' University of London, founded to get round the religious discrimination against Jews, dissenters and all those unwilling to sign the Thirty Nine Articles of the Church of England, provoked a great deal of opposition from the Establishment and the new University was mocked as 'The Cockney College'. The poet Winthrop Mackworth Praed wrote a spoof 'Discourse' delivered by a port-soaked Oxford college tutor to his peers in 1825 when the new University was being mooted:

Ye Dons and ye Doctors, ye Provosts and Proctors,
   Who are paid to monopolize knowledge,
Come, make opposition, by vote and petition,
   To the radical infidel college . . .

But let them not babble of Greek to the rabble,
   Nor teach the Mechanics their letters;
The labouring classes were born to be asses,
   And not to be aping their betters.[20]

The poem cleverly exposed the snobbish fear that the proposed London University would allow the lower orders into the sanctified world of learning. The Oxbridge dons in the poem are alarmed that 'fat butchers' and 'looking-glass makers' – tradesmen, in short – might be sending their sons (women's education still lagged behind and it was 1868 before the London Ladies' Educational Association was founded to provide classes for women and 1878 before women were admitted on the same footing as men) to learn medicine and philosophy. What is more, they would be nonconformists or even atheists ('sabbath-breakers') and the *lumpenproletariat* would be forsaking its usual pastimes for the seminar room ('The gin-shops are turn'd into cloisters').

To many of the readers of *The Morning Chronicle* where this poem first appeared on 19th July 1825, this was an unbearable thought. They need not have fretted, because today, 'UCL' is one of the most élitist parts of the British higher education system: a third of its places going to students from private fee-paying schools, one of the highest proportions of any British university. Less than one undergraduate in five has a working-class background. The Cockney rabble has been seen off.

A parrot called Wek

The poet Charlotte Mew was born at 10 Doughty Street in 1869, an address that today cries out for a blue plaque, but the family moved to 9 Gordon Street in 1888. No. 10 Doughty Street is the first of a little row of houses on the northern side of Guilford Street that start where the more splendid houses of Mecklenburgh Square, to which they are a sort of modest appendix, end. Doughty Street proper regains its magnificence once one has stepped back across Guilford Street to the south.

In Mecklenbugh Square there is a plaque to the Imagist poet H.D. (Hilda Dolittle) whose novel *Bid Me to Live* is set during the First World War in a fictionalised 'Queen's Square' (confusingly, because the real Queen Square has no apostrophe). Her husband, the poet Richard Aldington, wrote a more famous war novel, *Death of a Hero*, but H.D.'s book is the

more artistically interesting.

Mew is the best of the 'Bloomsbury born and bred' poets and Virginia Woolf told Vita Sackville West after meeting Mew that she judged her 'the greatest living poetess'.[21] Lady Ottoline Morrell also thought her 'the best of poets alive' but it was the admiration of Siegfried Sassoon and, even more, of Thomas Hardy, that meant most to Charlotte – though she was as far from the present day notion of the poet as celebrity as it is possible to be. Prevailed upon to attend a Poetry Book Shop reading in Bloomsbury she was greeted by the proprietor's wife and asked:

'Are you Charlotte Mew?' The downbeat reply
came: 'Yes, I'm afraid so.'

The Mews lived their life in genteel modesty
of means, especially after her father died when
she was 29. She wrote stories and poems and
was deeply attached to her sister whose death
affected her so much that she committed sui-
cide a year later in 1928. The novelist Penelope
Fitzgerald wrote a very fine biography, *Charlotte
Mew and her Friends*, which describes her unu-
sual if outwardly uneventful life.

The Mews kept a parrot called Wek and a fas-
cinated visitor once watched as Charlotte, who
liked a smoke, took one of the long paper spills
that she rolled to light her cigarettes and fed it
to the notoriously aggressive and bad-tempered
bird. There was a strong suspicion that these
spills were woven from abandoned manuscript
sheets of rejected poems.

In the 1920s the Euston Road was widened
opposite Euston Station and the Mews' house
at that end of Gordon Street was threatened.
Demolition began and great plane trees were
torn down by the developers. One of her finest
poems, 'The Trees Are Down', was prompted
by this destruction:

They are cutting down the great plane trees at the
      end of the gardens.
For days there has been the grate of the saw, the
      swish of the branches as they fall,
The crash of the trunks, the rustle of trodden
      leaves,
With the 'Whoops' and the 'Whoas,' the loud
      common talk, the loud common laughs of the
      men above it all.
[. . .]
It is going now, and my heart has been struck with
      the hearts of the planes;
Half my life it has beat with these, in the sun, in the
      rains.

All day, the poem concludes, she heard an angel crying: 'Hurt not the trees.'

Charlotte Mew, in a period that has been dominated by the celebrated male poets of the Great War, wrote her explicitly 'war' poems like 'May, 1915' ('Let us remember Spring will come again/ To the scorched, blackened woods, where the wounded trees/ Wait, with their old wise patience for the heavenly rain') and she is increasingly seen as one of the necessary voices of that era.

No more parades

M ew met and was admired by Siegfried Sassoon and another poet of the Great War, Wilfred Owen, who had signed up with the Artists' Rifles found himself learning drill in the commandeered Bloomsbury square, Cartwright Gardens. The Drill Hall of the Artists' Rifles still stands just off the Euston Road where it has become the home of The Space, a centre for contemporary dance.

Round the corner from the Drill Hall is Woburn Walk where the poet William Butler Yeats lived at No. 12 (then known as Woburn Buildings) from 1895 to 1919. He arrived in Bloomsbury from Dublin to rent a whole floor of No. 12 from an Irish connection. The charlady of Arthur Symons, the *fin de siècle* Irish poet and aesthete, mentioned that her husband had a flat to rent and Yeats moved in to where he would keep a salon on Monday nights and from where he reported that his sitting-room looked out 'on a raised flagged pavement where no traffic can come – & the bedroom very small & draughty, looks out on St Pancras Church with its caryatids & trees'.[22]

Today, Woburn Walk is rather an attractive architectural slice of Old Bloomsbury with an interesting mix of probably very expensive commercial properties cheek-by-jowl with cheap cafés. In Yeats's day it was also a down-to-earth passage and at No. 12 the attic was occupied by a pedlar and a cobbler lived on the floor below. A stonemason lived opposite. When he noticed that a blind beggar had situated himself like a *Big Issue* vendor outside, selling bootlaces and matches, Yeats concluded that all that was now needed was a pawnshop.

The formidable Lady Gregory, who figures largely in Yeats's story and that of the Celtic Revival, visited Woburn Walk some time after the poet had moved in and started to impose her sense of style on him. She presented him with a massive leather easy-chair and started work on the interior design: 'dim blues, tall white paschal candles, walls hung with brown paper, painted furniture, mystic hangings, prints and engravings by Blake, Rossetti, Beardsley,' writes his biographer, Roy Foster.[23] This very 1890s style was eclipsed, by the time Yeats was preparing to move out after the War in 1919, by black-painted floors and woodwork and orange hangings. When the poet Ezra Pound turned up he noted that Yeats had now 'painted the stairs sky blue'.

A stone's throw away, and while Yeats was still in residence (though there is no record of their having met), Wilfred Owen was mustering in the Drill Hall at No. 17 Duke's Road. The young poet arrived in Bloomsbury in October 1915 for training and was billeted in No. 54 Tavistock Square but the Bloomsbury style was not to his provincial taste: 'Tavistock Square,' he reported, 'is a replica of every other Bloomsbury Square; wadded with fog; skeletons of dismal trees behind the palings; but the usual west-end pervasion of ghostly aristocracy.'[24]

What Owen really wanted to do was to mix with the poets by taking the short walk to the far side of Queen Square, to Devonshire Street (now Boswell Street) to the legendary Poetry Bookshop (another mysteriously absent blue plaque) run by Harold Monro. Owen had tried to get lodgings over the shop, where the poet T. E. Hulme and the artist Jacob Epstein had succeeded, but was eventually forced to settle for rooms over the coffee shop opposite.

One war poet whom Owen did not meet was Isaac Rosenberg – a critic of Rupert Brooke's 'begloried sonnets'. Rosenberg attended Birkbeck College (not located in Bloomsbury at that time but in Fetter Lane) and later the Slade School of Art, just before the Great War. There are currently plans to erect a statue to Rosenberg in Torrington Square in Bloomsbury adjacent to Birkbeck College's present main entrance.

Routing the philistines

The Poetry Bookshop was in a flat-fronted Georgian house which was destroyed during the Blitz and in its place today, next door to the La Porchetta Italian restaurant, there is a hostel for homeless women. In the first couple of decades of the twentieth century Harold Monro's Poetry Bookshop was at the centre of a poetic revolution. The old order, represented by the fag end of Victorianism, was yielding to a new century's desire for less vagueness and more realism and more exactitude in poetic language and image.

Two movements, the Georgians and the Imagists, formed the avant-garde and Monro, a canny operator, managed to cater to both. The later poets of the 1930s, such as MacNiece and Spender, sneered at the Georgians as pastoral weekenders writing insipid verse, but the Georgians themselves, like Robert Graves or Rupert

Brooke, saw themselves as being in the vanguard of the new poetry.

It was only a short distance away, just across the Bloomsbury boundary in Raymond Buildings, Gray's Inn, that Brooke and his patron Edward Marsh had drawn up the movement's blueprint, the annual *Georgian Poetry* anthologies which were to showcase the new departure in verse.

Imagism, though some poets like D. H. Lawrence managed to fit comfortably into both movements' anthologies, was a more austere Modernist project, with polemical manifestos setting out detailed aesthetic programmes and principles. As the label suggests they felt the way for poetry to escape the old sonorous waffle was to focus on the clear, hard outline of the poetic image and strip away everything that was deemed unnecessary. The result, unsurprisingly, was a pared down, rather minimalist poetry that now in retrospect looks a little thin.

Bloomsbury resident poets like T. E. Hulme and H.D. became Imagism's chief proponents and Monro happily stocked both anthologies in the shop at No. 35 where poetry browsers used to listen to the soft thud of gold-beaters' hammers from the workshop next door (now La Porchetta).

On the night of 11th July 1913, after the notorious first London performance of Stravinsky's *Le Sacre du printemps*, all the progressive spirits in the poetry world flocked to the Poetry Bookshop to celebrate that triumphant routing of the conservative musical old guard.

Monro made the Poetry Bookshop a place where everyone wanted to read. In a dimly lit annexe behind the shop he put on T. S. Eliot, Robert Graves, Ezra Pound, Walter de la Mare, and just about anyone who counted in the world of poetry. Only Yeats proved too much of draw and had to be put on at the Artificers' Guild Hall in adjacent Queen Square (now the Art Workers' Guild).

The shop was located in a rough area where the policemen preferred to patrol in pairs and the street urchins ran along behind Rupert Brooke when he arrived in his characteristic broad-brimmed hat chanting: 'Buffalo Bill! Buffalo Bill!' Sir Osbert Sitwell, in his elegant suit and canary yellow waistcoat, was another target for the derision of these scallywags. Afterwards he described Devonshire Street as 'a narrow street . . . rather dark, but given over to screaming children, lusty small boys armed with catapults, and to leaping flights of cats'.[25]

Monro's neighbour on the other side, a boisterous flower seller at Piccadilly Circus, handed Monro's propitiatory gift of some children's poetry books to her yobbish boys, who eagerly tore them to pieces and stamped them into the ground.

Of Ted and Sylvia

I t was in Queen Square, on 'Bloomsday' on 16th June 1956, that a young poet called Ted Hughes married his American wife, Sylvia Plath, at the church of St George-the-Martyr, a few yards from the former site of the Poetry Bookshop. It was at the height of austerity Britain with Hughes wearing his one utility suit. The bride's mother was present but no one else and the couple had to drag in the sexton, who was just preparing to lead a party of children to a zoo trip, to be a witness.

The event is described in Hughes's poem 'A Pink Wool Knitted Dress' in his collection *Birthday Letters*. Hughes called the church 'St George of the Chimney Sweeps', because the Victorian child sweeps used to be treated to a Christmas dinner there, recalling how they exchanged rings in 'that echo-gaunt, weekday chancel'.[26]

In another poem in that collection, '18 Rugby Street', Hughes describes the house at No. 18 Rugby Street where he rented an apartment in the late 1950s. There was no water to each flat, only cold water on the landings, an outside lavatory at the bottom, and the only bath one could get was at the public facilities at Holborn Baths.

On the night of March 23, 1956, Hughes had spent his first night here with Sylvia Plath before she left for Paris the next day, an event commemorated by his poem which refers to the 'Victorian torpor and squalor' of No. 18 which was in multiple occupation and on each of the four floors the tenants bed-hopped in a 'laboratory of amours'.

A Belgian girl in the ground-floor flat entertained a second-hand car dealer and stored for him his exhaust silencers and car parts. Hughes sat here alone writing at an old joiner's bench that served as desk and table and it was here that he and Plath spent their wedding night in the single bed.

The earthly paradise

Queen Square's long eastern side is almost entirely occupied now by hospital buildings but in the 1860s, at No. 25, the poet William Morris had the headquarters of his weaving workshop. Morris & Co arrived in Queen Square in 1865 from Red Lion Square and had their company HQ here for the next seventeen years.

Like so many Bloomsbury businesses Morris worked with the constraints of a Georgian house to convert it into an office and show-room on the ground floor and turned the former ballroom at the back, which was connected to the main house by a wooden gallery, into the chief workshop. More overspill workshops were in time built to the yards at the rear and in Ormond Yard. While he was here launching his new tapestry-weaving line, William Morris wrote *The Life and Death of Jason* and *The Earthly Paradise*.

Slipping out of Queen Square along Cosmo Place into Southampton Row one steps back into the eighteenth century, trying to work out where the lodgings of the poet Thomas Gray might have been in the middle of that century. On 24th July 1759 Gray, wrote to his friend William Palgrave:[27]

I am now settled in my new territories commanding Bedford Gardens, and all the fields as far as Highgate and Hampstead, with such a concourse of moving pictures as would astonish you; so *rus-in-urbe*-ish, that I believe I shall stay here, except little excursions and vagaries, for a year to come. What though I am separated from the fashionable world by broad St Giles's, and many a dirty court and alley, yet here is air and sunshine, and quiet, however, to comfort you: I shall confess that I am basking with heat all summer, and I suppose shall be blown down all the winter, besides being robbed every night; I trust, however, that the Museum, with all its manuscripts and rarities by the cart-load, will make ample amends for all the aforesaid inconveniences.

Gray's letter reminds us that Bloomsbury prior to the explosion of development after 1800 was indeed rather rural with open fields punctuated with duck ponds running north of Great Russell Street to Hampstead and Highgate. To the West were the notorious 'rookeries' of St Giles where the poet was right to be apprehensive about being robbed and on the far side of which 'the fashionable world' might be found in the West End.

For Gray there was the consolation of the newly opened British Museum but this building put another poet early in the following century in a more angry mood.

Lord Byron was furious at the presence of Lord Elgin's collection of marbles or 'misshapen monuments' captured from the Parthenon and installed in the Museum. In his poem 'Childe Harold's Pilgrimage' he lamented:

> Dull is the eye that will not weep to see
> Thy walls defaced, thy mouldering shrines removed
> By British hands, which it had best behoved
> To guard those relics ne'er to be restored.
> Curst be the hour when from their isle they roved,
> And once again thy hapless bosom gored,
> And snatch'd thy shrinking gods to northern climes
>   abhorred!

Controversy has always dogged the Marbles, especially in regard to their treatment by the British Museum over the years. Quite apart from the damage from London's nineteenth-century pollution ('northern climes abhorred') there were some disastrous attempts in the 1930s to clean the fifth-century BC pentelic marble with scrapers and various solutions. The BM mandarins reply that Athens itself is a polluted city and they might have fared no better there.

The debate remains polarised between an idea that there is a special iconic quality to the Parthenon marbles necessitating their restoration to their original setting in Greece and the belief that London does these things better, displaying them in a context where they may be appreciated globally (with the invisible rider, one always feels, that Athens is some sort of provincial outpost inhabited by excitable foreigners like the actress and former culture minister Melina Mercouri, in her day one of the more impassioned and memorable advocates of restitution).

It was in a building which is now the site of the British Museum's Director's residence at the western end of Great Russell Street that the seventeenth-century poet Andrew Marvell died. No one (including his biographer[28]) is absolutely certain what happened but it seems that the medical treatment he received for an 'ague' was rather heavy-handed, involving sweating and bleeding the patient who, after these exertions, died on Friday 16th August 1678 in a coma.

Marvell had taken out a lease on the Great Russell Street property in this rapidly developing part of London, in the name of the woman who may or may not have been his wife, Mary Palmer, to help a pair of dodgy bankers on the run from their creditors in Hull and was, as so often, in his shady life living incognito and at the edge of things. His memorial is in St Giles-in-the-Fields church just outside the Bloomsbury boundary.

Let's sing ourselves out with the jauntiest, if not the most poetically distinguished, Bloomsbury poem, published in 1906 in the *Pall Mall Magazine*. Written by the poet John Davidson, whose satirical ballad 'Thirty Bob a Week' is probably better known, it celebrates Bloomsbury and its garden squares:

> What? Russell Square!
> There's lilac there!
> And Torrington
> And Woburn Square
> Intrepid don
> The season's wear.
> In Gordon Square and Euston Square –
> There's lilac, there's laburnum there!
> In green and gold and lavender.
> Queen Square and Bedford Square,
> All Bloomsbury and all Soho
> With every sunbeam gayer grow,
> Greener grow and gayer.

Notes

1 Cited by Victoria Glendinning in *Vita: The life of V. Sackville-West* (1983), p.186. That was in 1927; in 1943 she observed : 'I think it sounds dreadful. The proletariat being encouraged to breed like rabbits because each new little rabbit means 8/- a week – as though there weren't too many of them already . . .', p.320.

2 Paul Ferris (ed.), *The Collected Letters of Dylan Thomas* (1985), p.56.

3 Harold Nicholson, *The Bloomsbury Group* (2009), The British Library, NSACD-58-59.

4 Henry James, *Collected Travel Writings* (New York, Library of America, 1993), 'English Hours', p.36. Original edition 1888.

5 Ford Madox Ford, *The Soul of London* (1905), Everyman edition, 1995, p.7.

6 V. S. Pritchett, *London Perceived* (1986), p.168.

7 Ian Nairn, *Nairn's London* (1966), p.96.

8 Vanessa Bell, *Sketches in Pen and Ink* (1997), p.110.

9 Roy Campbell, *Light on a Dark Horse* (1971), p.194. See also Nicholas Murray, *Aldous Huxley:*

an English Intellectual (2003), p.126.

10 Roy Campbell, *The Georgiad* (1931).

11 Rimbaud, *Oeuvres Complètes* (Paris, 1972).

12 Jean Cocteau, *Paris* (Paris, 2013), p.13.

13 Virginia Woolf, cited in *The Story of Marchmont Street* (2008) by Ricci de Freitas, p.30.

14 *Selected Letters of William Empson* (2006), p.12.

15 Cited by John Haffenden, *William Empson: Among the Mandarins* (2005), p.261.

16 Ibid. See also, Nicholas Murray, *Real Bloomsbury* (2010), pp.65–6.

17 *The Letters of T. S. Eliot*, Volume 1, 1898–1922, p.xvii.

18 Louis MacNeice, *Collected Poems* (2007), edited by Peter McDonald, p.591.

19 Christopher Reid, *The Song of Lunch* (2009), p.4.

20 Kenneth Allott (ed.), *Selected Poems of Winthrop Mackworth Praed* (1953), pp.276–7.

21 For all these citations see Penelope Fitzgerald, *Charlotte Mew and Her Friends* (1984) and Val Warner (ed.), *Charlotte Mew: Collected Poems and Prose* (1981).

22 Roy Foster, *W. B. Yeats: A Life*, I: *The Apprentice Mage* (1997), p.161.

23 Roy Foster, *W. B. Yeats: A Life*, II: *The Arch-Poet* (2003), p.83.

24 Wilfred Owen, *Selected Letters* (1985), edited by John Bell, p.167.

25 See Nicholas Murray, *Real Bloomsbury* (2010) and

The Red Sweet Wine of Youth for a fuller account of the Poetry Bookshop.

26 Ted Hughes, *Birthday Letters* (1998).

27 *Letters of Thomas Gray* (1925), edited by John Beresford, p.191.

28 See Nicholas Murray, *World Enough and Time: The Life of Andrew Marvell* (1999), p.252.

Index

Rack Press Editions was launched in 2014.
It is an imprint of **Rack Press Poetry**, a poetry
pamphlet press founded in 2005, which has published
more than thirty contemporary poets in quality
limited editions

'Rack Press ever impresses' – *Poetry Review*
'The consistently reliable Rack Press'
– *Times Literary Supplement*